# CARPETS FROM THE ORIENT

# IN THE SAME SERIES

Translated from the
Dutch by Marieke Clarke

# Carpets

## from the

# Orient

## by J. M. Con

UNIVERSE BOOKS INC.
381 Park Avenue South
New York, New York 10016

The original edition of this book was published in The Netherlands
by van Dishoeck, van Holkema & Warendorf N.V.

First printing

Published in the United States of America by

UNIVERSE BOOKS, Inc.
381 Park Avenue South
New York, N.Y. 10016

Library of Congress Catalog Card Number: 65—24048

Printed in The Netherlands

# Contents

# The history of the oriental carpet

Every admirer of oriental carpets wants to know which ones are antique, how old they are, and how to tell the age of a carpet. Though these are obvious questions, it is difficult to answer them satisfactorily. It is true that there are people, usually dealers, who can tell the age of a carpet to within ten years. But if we ask these people on what evidence they base their judgment, we usually receive very vague answers; sometimes the experts keep quiet and are unable to reply. Yet it is true that it is often very difficult to give an approximate date to an antique carpet. When experts disagree about the age of a carpet and differ by more than a century in their estimate, we can be satisfied to divide carpets into antique, old and modern carpets.

## Antique carpets

A carpet woven before the middle of the 19th century which is of aesthetic or historic value is antique. Long before the beginning of the Christian era the art of making carpets was fully developed in the East.

The oldest known carpets were discovered in 1949 by the Russian archaeologists Rudenko and Grjansnov. They found the carpets in the valley of the Pazyrik, about 5,000 feet up on the Altai Mountains in Siberia. These archaeologists found the tombs of Scythian chiefs with their servants and horses, in a family vault. The grave was 2,400 or 2,500 years old and its contents had been frozen and thus preserved as if in a refrigerator. Two carpets (now in Leningrad) were found as well as weapons and furs. One carpet about 20 by 13 feet, was made of felt against which horsemen and a

7

goddess on a throne were appliqued in the same material. The other carpet, a very fine one, is knotted. It is about five by six feet. It was found on a horse's back and must have been used as a saddle. The carpet is made in the same way as a modern hand-knotted carpet with a woollen warp, weft and pile and a Turkish knot. There are 240 knots per square inch. Its colours are red, blue, yellowish green and orange.

A few fragments of carpets have survived from the 12th and 13th centuries A.D. Obviously carpets suffer much more wear and tear than stone statues and antique bronzes, which, as everyone knows, show the passage of time. Any silver bracelet that is a hundred years old, and regularly worn, shows its age; so it is not surprising that there are only a few carpets with a history of 700 or 800 years.

Although carpets of this age are rare, there is quite a large number of fine examples dating from the 16th and 17th centuries. Most of these are beautifully made and have lovely colours and designs. But it would be wrong to deduce that every carpet made in the 16th or 17th century was a masterpiece, just because we hardly ever see mediocre ones. These masterpieces were preserved simply because they were valuable even at the time they were made. They were treated with more care than the ordinary carpets which must have been produced and it is for this reason that the fine carpets which beautify many of our museums have survived.

The 16th-17th centuries in Persia were a Golden Age for all forms of artistic expression, not only carpet weaving. The Sefavid dynasty were generous but discriminating patrons and Shah Abbas who reigned from 1586—1628 was among the most brilliant of his line. The Sefavids like their contemporaries, the Sultans of Turkey, had their own carpet factories in which hundreds of workers constantly produced the most magnificent carpets for their rulers. When the carpets were not hung in the palaces of the monarchs, they were presented to favourites, dignitaries, mosques, foreign ambassadors or friendly rulers in the West. And because these gifts were valued very highly they were likely to be preserved for future generations. Although we know very little about it, a village carpet weaving industry probably existed as well as the one at the court.

Fine carpets appear in many paintings of the 16th and 17th centuries. In the 16th century paintings these carpets are usually from Asia Minor or Anatolia — one type of Anatolian carpet is even called 'Holbein carpet' because it appears so often in his paintings. In the 17th century Persian carpets begin to appear as well and a very distinctive type of Ushak carpet instead of the earlier 'Holbein carpets'. Rembrandt and Frans Hals often depicted carpets and many interesting carpets appear in Dutch still life paintings, often on tables, sometimes draped to show the pattern to advantage.

Even the best preserved pieces in museums turn out on close inspection to be very fragmentary, since they are usually torn and repaired and full of holes. The fact that even in this state they can make us wonder at their beauty only increases our admiration for the art of the oriental carpet makers.

The best way to learn about antique carpets is to go to see them in museums, or in private collections which are open to the public. Descriptions and illustrations of antique carpets are no substitute for seeing the real thing. There are good collections of carpets in the Metropolitan Museum of Art in New York, in the Textile Museum in Washington and in many other leading American museums. In Europe collections which should be visited include those in Vienna (in the Oesterreichisches Museum für Angewandte Kunst), and in London (in the Victoria and Albert Museum). Two of the most famous carpets in the world from the Mosque at Ardabil can be found: one in the Victoria and Albert Museum and the pair to it in the Los Angeles County Museum of Art.

## Old carpets

Old carpets are those made from the middle to the end of the 19th century. Very valuable carpets were still made after 1800, but they show obvious signs of a decline. The patterns became stiffer and less graceful. The colours were not matched with such good taste and the rich, distinguished-looking shades of the antique carpets were replaced by harder, brighter, less subtle dyes. The year 1859 was a fatal one for the carpet-weavers' art because, in that year, aniline dyes were discovered and were very quickly exported to the East. The discovery of aniline dyes was disastrous for they were fugitive, neither fast to light nor to water, and their tones were completely discordant with those of the softer natural dyes still in use. Modern synthetic dyes are generally fast and their colours need not be any more strident than those of natural dyestuffs. Coal tar dyes were cheap and easy to use but of such poor quality that it was impossible to make a good carpet with them.

Even so, good carpets were made in the 19th century. There had always been many carpets produced for everyday use as well as those made for their artistic value. The latter can be regarded as folk art in every sense. These carpets were not made by specialists but by peasants, shepherds and hunters for their own use but they were made with great care and attention. Because the craftsman usually made his carpets of home-spun yarn from his own sheep, the carpets are usually of excellent quality. Since people often devote more care and use more of their imagination in creating something for themselves than for other people, the carpets frequently astonish us because of the freshness of the colours and the richness of the pattern. Vegetable dyes were most frequently used on a softly lustrous wool. Nomad carpets are often masterpieces of folk art. Few of these rugs survive and although a few years ago it was fairly easy to gather together a fine collection of them, they have now become so scarce that it is probable that in twenty or thirty years time they will have disappeared from the market. The further western culture penetrates to the East, the quicker the ancient oriental culture declines as a result of mechanisation. Anyone who can buy a nomad rug should do so now . . .

Old carpets can be distinguished from antiques, although one can never determine the actual age because in the East fashions do not change. A nomad woman who knots a carpet today does so in exactly the same way as her great-grand-mother. She uses the same sort of wool, the same dyes, the same techniques, the same simple loom and the same patterns as her ancestress.

Nor does the age of the carpet matter. For a true lover of carpets it is unimportant if a carpet is showing signs of age so long as it has a good colour, is well woven and carefully knotted, with a stylish pattern, good design, good quality wool and is dyed with vegetable dyes.

## Modern carpets

Modern carpets are those made in the 20th century using contemporary techniques. They are made for export and their production is purely a commercial undertaking. For the dealers these carpets are the ones that matter, and without them there would be no trade. For Persia, especially, but for other main eastern countries as well, carpets are the largest export, and more than half of the population derives its living directly or indirectly from them.

Although some people set little store by modern carpets, some very good carpets are produced. It is true that poor quality carpets are exported to Europe and there are both good and bad carpet manufacturers.

Immediately after 1900 some people in the East thought that Europeans and Americans would buy any carpet, how-ever poor the quality, but fortunately this is no longer the case. The Persian carpet weaving industry has grown wise through experience and finding that its warehouses were full of vast supplies of unsaleable rubbish because the West refused to buy inferior carpets, changed its policy and improved its standards. The industry was saved from complete disaster by a rise in the standard of products assisted by regulations laid down by the Persian government. These regulations forbade the use of inferior dyes and set certain standards that had to be observed regarding the tension and the quality of the wool. So it became possible to re-establish the carpet industry; as a result Persian carpets have regained their former reputation. The people of the Orient continue to make superb carpets as they did in the past.

In the West machines for the weaving of carpets have been invented which are ingenious and highly efficient but not even the most perfect machine can produce carpets to rival the imaginative, rich and yet essentially simple oriental rug.

# How are oriental carpets made?

Oriental carpets can be divided into three groups according to the way in which they are made. There are the kelims, which are smooth, have no pile and are nearly the same on both sides. A sumak rug is also without a knotted pile but is woven with a herring-bone effect on the face and many loose ends on the back of the rug. Knotted carpets have pile and are smooth on the reverse side.

It is easy to distinguish one sort of carpet from another, but many admirers do not know how the carpets are made. Although every book on carpets includes at least one chapter on the technique of making them, readers usually omit to read that chapter. But everyone who is interested in carpets ought to know how they are made so that he can find out where they come from, and whether they are made by hand or not.

The *kelim* is tapestry woven but made on a loom similar to that used for carpets woven with a knotted pile. This consists of two wooden beams held apart by cross beams. Between these two beams are stretched at tension a series of parallel threads forming the warp. If the warp threads are thin and are close together the material is fine. If the warp threads are thick and far apart, the material is coarse. Counting from left to right on the loom, one can divide the threads into those which are even and those which are odd numbers. The division of these two sets of threads is called the shed. The weaver lifts all the even threads together in one line of weaving and all the odd threads on the next. He throws his shuttle (on which is the weft) across the loom for each line. He beats the weft down as he works so that the threads are as close together as possible. This method will produce the simplest possible woven material. By using different colours

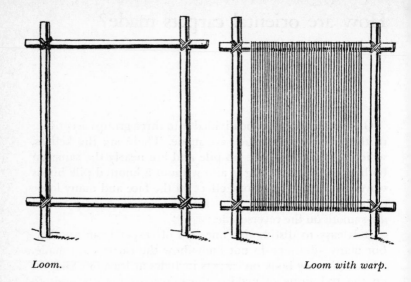

Loom.                                                    Loom with warp.

and this method, craftsmen can produce striped patterns. In
order to make a pattern of squares which are alternately red
and blue, and ten warp threads wide, a shuttle with a red
thread is passed under five even threads and over five odd
threads. The weaver turns his shuttle back at this point and
in the next shed returns over the five odd threads and under
the even ones.

A shuttle with a blue thread is then used in the same way
on the next ten threads. The warp is completely covered by
the wefts beaten down upon each other. Between the red and
blue squares there is a gap unless the adjacent red and blue
wefts have been linked around each other or around the same
warp thread. The gaps formed between two colours are,
however, typical of a tapestry woven fabric and are often
used to emphasise decorative effects. The material on both
sides is similar, provided that all the ends of the wool have
been carefully finished off. The same method of weaving

14

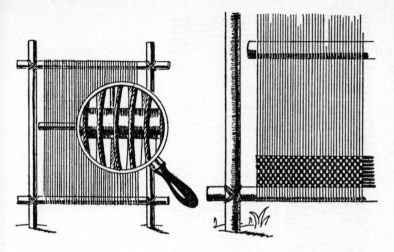

*Loom with warp and weft.*     *Loom with kelim.*

can be used to make much more complicated patterns, although we have only described the making of a simple pattern in squares. But there are certain limitations imposed on anyone who uses the kelim technique. Round or curved lines cannot be woven. Most kelims have rectangular geometrical shapes. Persian *sinneh-kelims* are a notable exception to this rule but they demand very great technical skill. There is another disadvantage if one uses the kelim technique. Long straight lines are difficult to manage because too long a gap cannot be left in the fabric without weakening it.

*Sumak* rugs are made on a similar loom but with a different technique. The weft which makes the pattern is taken over four threads and back under two. Like the weft in the kelim it is only taken the distance of the motif in the pattern. Between each line of sumak the weaver passes one or more wefts right across the loom. No gaps are left between adjacent

15

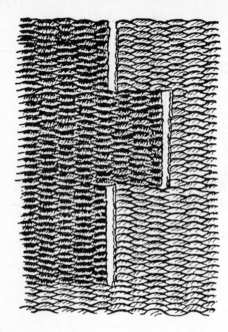

*Fragment of a kelim showing the gaps.*

colours, and the loose ends at the edges of the motifs in the pattern are left floating on the back of the fabric. On an old carpet these loose ends may have become very ragged.

*Knotted carpets* are made on similar looms. After a few wefts have been woven to make a firm end to the carpet knotting can begin. There are two different kinds of knots, the *ghiordes* or *Turkish knot* and the *sinneh* or *Persian knot*.

To tie a ghiordes knot, a thread is laid across two warp threads and the ends are drawn forward between them. For a sinneh knot, one single warp thread is entirely surrounded and the wool is wound half round the next one. Threads for the pile can be cut beforehand and measured, or cut through later.

When a row of knots has been tied across the width, they

*1. Sinneh-kelim (west Persia).*

*2. Feraghan (central Persia).*

*3. Serabend (north-west Persia).*

*4. Kerman (east Persia).*

*5. Saruk (central Persia).*

6. *Mosul (borders of west Persia)*.

*7. Saveh (Hamadan district, central Persia).*

*8. Bakhtiari (south Persia).*

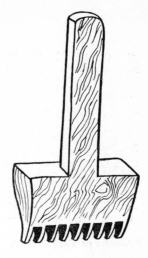

*Comb used for beating down the weft.*

are beaten down using a heavy iron comb and one or more wefts passed across the loom before the next row is knotted. This ensures that the material is firm. The number of weft threads can vary considerably and the more that are made, the thicker the carpet becomes.

Usually the carpet is knotted following a pattern which is

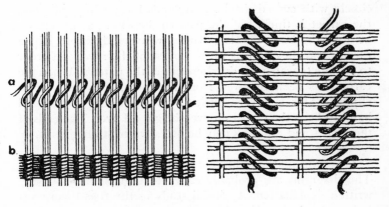

*Sumak technique.*

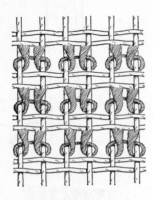

*Ghiordes or Turkish knot.*

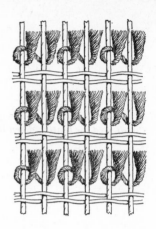

*Sinneh or Persian knot.*

made beforehand and hung beside the loom. The pattern may not be detailed enough to show every knot but an experienced carpet weaver takes care to follow the pattern, even though the carpet may show slight irregularities.

The balls of thread for the pile are hung on the loom. After a knot has been tied the end is cut off and generally when three or four rows have been tied the ends are cut more closely with curved shears. Long ends form a high pile and the carpet is thick, but the pattern does not emerge clearly because the ends lie flat. Carpet weavers therefore clip a carpet, and they do this in the course of their work in order to be able to watch the development of the pattern. When the carpet has been removed from the loom, it is once again clipped. This is a very difficult task requiring a practised hand to keep the carpet an even height all over. The ends of the carpet and the sides may be oversewn to strengthen it.

This sums up the technique of the different types of carpet. The diagrams are probably easier to understand than any written explanation. A careful study of the rugs themselves is, however, better than either.

# Colours and dyes

The dyes used to colour the wool are of the greatest importance in completing the effect and lengthening the life of oriental carpets. Innumerable raw materials have been used to dye wool and dyers have always been greatly respected.

Most of the traditional raw materials were of vegetable origin: roots, flowers, bark and leaves; also employed were some animal products and various insects. The preparation of dyestuffs varied from family to family.

We understand why there may be slight variations even in one colour when we know how the dyes are prepared. After the wool has been washed and dried it is dipped into a pot of dye until it achieves the right colour. The wool is then hung above the pot to dry, and later washed in cold water before being hung in the sun on a flat roof to dry. In Asia Minor the dyer's home is always immediately to be recognised by the brightly coloured wool on his roof. Thorough precautions cannot prevent different vegetable matter or different treatment producing slight variations in colour so that a carpet weaver who has insufficient wool of a colour to complete his work will sometimes find that there are differences when he buys new wool of the same colour.

Blue and red are the colours which remain fast longest and in the course of time they become mellow. Brown often loses its gloss as it gets older and black is an unreliable colour. It is prepared, not from vegetable matter, but from iron filings and gall-nut which eventually damages the wool. Many antique carpets have survived undamaged except for the black wool which is generally badly worn. Natural brown or black wool, or brown camel-hair, is used where possible instead of artificially dyed material. The best red dye is carmine or 'kermes' which is made from insects found on one particular sort of oak tree. It is said that this shade of red was known even at the time of Moses. Cochineal is another very popular red dye, made from greenfly found on cacti. Many red dyes are made using madder. Indigo is used to make blue and if the wool is dipped in other colours as well all sorts of lovely shades can be obtained. Green is obtained by dipping the wool first in yellow and then in indigo. Many different plants native to the area are used to obtain yellow shades; of these saffron is best known in the West. Later the bark of the quercitron tree was used. Brown is often made from madder and yellow, but other materials, such as gall-nut and husks of walnut, are often used. 'Logwood' from Central America is frequently employed as a vegetable basis for a black dye.

The popular belief that vegetable dyes, in contrast to chemical dyes, do not fade is unfounded. When vegetable dyes fade, however, they become softer and more attractive.

Analine dyes spread rapidly in the East since they were cheaper, simpler to prepare and easier to use than natural dyes. They included a large number of bright colours which were popular both in the East and with their Western customers.

In Persia the government forbade the import and use of aniline dyes in 1900 and threatened to cut off the right hand of anyone who imported or used chemical dyes. But the law was never strictly enforced and many aniline dyes are used; even in Kerman, Khorosan, Kurdistan and in many other areas where vegetable dyes are still used, aniline dyes are becoming increasingly popular.

In Asia Minor, on the other hand, no government action has been taken against the use of chemical dyes. At least three-quarters of the wool is dyed with aniline. Some chemical colours are faster than natural colours; they may, however, in some cases affect the wool adversely. A carpet dyed with bad artificial dyes may wear out more quickly in consequence.

The chemical dyes of modern carpets may be very harsh in tone. Acid is used to correct this fault, and the factories, most of them in London, are expert in rinsing in acid. Very harshly coloured carpets become softer and have a very deceptive gloss after this treatment.

Each people has its own favourite colours; Persians prefer dark green and yellow, the Turks like red and the Armenians choose blue. Turks use little green since this is for them a holy colour, the colour of the Prophet's flag; walking on this colour would be desecration. This is the reason why green is usually used by Turks in prayer rugs.

# Motif and symbol in the oriental carpet

It is impossible to include in one chapter all that is known about symbolism in oriental carpets. Many people who are interested in and know much about carpets know nothing about the meaning of the symbols, and are indeed often unaware of their existence.

Originally every motif, decoration and colour on a carpet had a symbolic significance, but the original meaning is now often forgotten as a result of the change in design. Many decorations are extremely old and were first used in pre-historic times. Different colours had varying symbolic significance: dark blue represented eternity in Persia, misfortune in India, and power in China. Since the motifs explain a great deal about the carpets, and about the people who made them, a short explanation is included here of the meaning of some of the most common decorations.

*Zigzag edge:* it appears in all carpets, but especially in Caucasian ones. It symbolises running water, which in turn symbolises eternity.

*Hour glass:* this symbolises time and eternity.

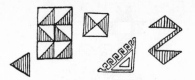

*Triangle:* earth symbol. In India it means good luck.

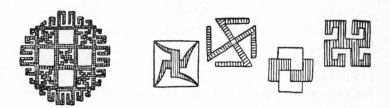

*Swastika:* means good fortune, abundance, fertility and prosperity. It occurs in even the oldest cultures. The Greeks, the Egyptians, the Chinese, the Incas, and the earliest cave dwellers all had it but the motif occurs most frequently in Chinese and Caucasian carpets.

*'S' ornament:* symbol of the sun-god for sun-worshippers. The motif also represents the snake as the symbol of wisdom.

*The cross:* for Moslems this never has a religious significance.

*Eight-pointed star:* the symbols of Solomon, and Mohammed's jewel.

*Six-pointed star:* the sign of David, adopted by Moslems as a talisman.

Both star motifs appear in Caucasian and Turkoman carpets.

*Sunband motif:* symbol of the life-giving power of the sun. It appears only in Caucasian carpets, especially in sumaks.

*Cypress:* the tree of life. This evergreen symbolises eternal life. It appears especially in Persian carpets.

*Lily:* the favourite flower of the Indians. It symbolises innocence and purity.

*Lotus:* the waterlily, the holy flower of the Egyptians,

24

Assyrians and Indians. It symbolises purity and immortality; for the Chinese it symbolises fertility.

*Pomegranate:* symbol of fertility and the blessing of children.

*Weeping willow:* symbol of death. It frequently appears in 'cemetery' carpets, so-called because of their decoration.

*Shawl motif:* it is called 'Flower of the Shahs' by the Persians. Some authorities say that it is a fir cone, a symbol of long life, others say that it represents a fist, often used by early rulers as a seal. The symbol is the most common of all those appearing in Eastern carpets and appears very frequently in Persian ones.

*Jug and comb:* these two motifs appear together, and in prayer rugs they appear many times over. They are intended to remind the faithful that they must wash before they pray.

*Cloud band:* this was originally a Chinese motif, but the Persians adopted it. Originally it was a Buddhist design, and it symbolises the principle of life, immortality and the seat of divinity.

*Scorpion:* the bite of a scorpion is very dangerous, and for many nomad tribes in the Caucasus and Central Asia it symbolises defence.

*Dragon:* for Persians the dragon was the symbol of evil and destruction. In China it was a sacred animal. It symbolises infinity, guardian of treasure, and imperial power.

*Dog:* represents dependence and trust, and often appears in stylised form in nomad carpets.

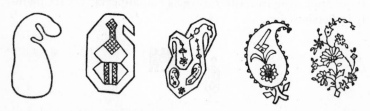

*Serabend motif* (Boteh Miri): this motif, which is known by many names, appears more often than any other in India, Persia and Europe. It is not difficult to imagine how the

design must have developed, each craftsman adding to the original design.

*Herati motif:* Herat is a town in the north of Afghanistan, and belonged at one time to Persia. It was famous for the magnificent carpets that were made there. The herati pattern was a unique one, much admired and sought after. Thousands of herat carpets were hung in Persian mosques, thousands were exported to India, Turkey and Europe. Herat carpets were

of such excellent quality that the weavers were unable to fulfil all their orders and they became very rich.

Their success aroused jealousy, especially among the carpet weavers of Feraghan and Khorassan, and, because there were no copyright laws in those days, people began to imitate the herati pattern. The motif changed as it was copied until the

herati design appeared in one form or another in practically every sort of carpet in the Near East.

27

The pattern is too complicated to describe in detail but it may be illustrated.

The border of the herat carpets also had an individual character: even today many carpets are made with the herati motif, but with the centre design completely altered. The typical herati border consisted of alternate rosettes and lancet-shaped leaves, as the illustrations show.

# Persian carpets

Little has so far been said about the genuine Persian
carpets. These are perhaps the most famous, because of their
richness of colour. The carpets are made in the uplands of
Persia, where there is green only in springtime, and the land
is very poor.

Knotted carpets and kelims are both made in Persia; the
latter are mainly used to decorate the walls and to lay on
divans. The so-called 'Polonaise' carpets, which were made in
Persia and exported to Poland to the orders of the Polish
nobility are very interesting. They often bear the coats of
arms of Polish families and it was not until the 19th century
that they were recognised as Persian. Their patterns are very
fine and their pile is usually silk. Large areas of the pattern
are not, however, carried out in knotted pile but are brocad-
ed in gold or silver thread. This gives a sumptuous effect,
even though the silver thread may be tarnished and the pile
worn.

Ispahan was a renowned centre for the weaving of carpets
when it was the capital city of Shah Abbas and it continued
to be celebrated until it was sacked in 1722. There was then
a complete break in its traditional crafts. Carpet weaving
was revived in the present century but during the 19th
century the city was a trade centre to which carpets were
brought for sale from the villages where they were made.
Ispahan, like many other towns thus gave its name to various
types of carpet among them a type with pile knotted on both
sides. Persian carpets knotted exactly the same way on both
sides are rare, but they can still be found. They were probably
used instead of screens to divide a room in two. A carpet of
an even rarer sort was discovered in 1900 in Teheran, but
has since disappeared. It was a prayer rug, with both sides

knotted, one with wool and the other with silk. The patterns were different.

Sometimes Persian carpets were clipped in such a way that certain colours stood out further than others. This gives an attractive effect like relief, as in very old carpets when certain coloured wools rot sooner than others.

There is no producer of carpets with such a variety of patterns as the Persian, and each area of Persia had its own designs. The most common Persian motifs are those with flowers, linked by tendrils, and designs including animals and human beings; partly geometrical motifs are also common. These are often found on kelims. Weavers in Sinneh make kelims, however, with graceful curvilinear designs. Garden scenes are quite common on Persian carpets, and show not only the flower-beds, streams and paths, but also the birds and wild animals. While the effect is that of a complete garden, the motifs are rendered without natural perspective so that the decorative effect suitable to a carpet is preserved. Later imitations of these carpets are not always successful. Indeed, distorted versions of garden and hunting carpets can be very ugly. Particularly deplorable are certain pictorial carpets with designs showing ancient Assyrian warriors, famous modern heroes, architecturally impossible buildings, or deformed lions and tigers. Aesthetic sensibility has varied in different regions. In some more attention had been paid to the pattern, in others to the colouring.

Persian carpets are usually made of wool. The finest wool is shorn in the spring from the bellies of sheep and goats. This wool is long, soft and silky. 'Kush', as it is called, is the most sought-after wool in Persia, although there are many different varieties. In the region of Hamadan and Kurdistan camel-hair is sometimes used. Silk is frequently employed to make very finely knotted carpets, but it is expensive and does not wear as well as wool. Silk carpets do not attract moths; such carpets were always handled with great care and old ones therefore often survive.

The sinneh knot is the one most commonly used for Persian carpets. The most coarsely knotted carpets come from Kurdistan and the finest from Kashan. Persian carpets can be subdivided into five main types according to size.

Rooms in Persia are usually long and narrow; this accounts for the size of the carpets. The rooms are divided as is shown in the diagram:

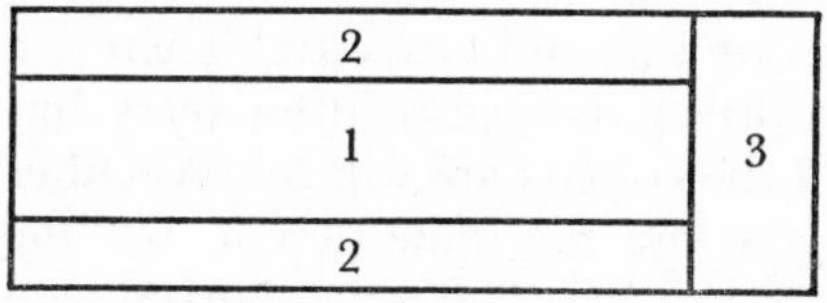

| 2 | |
|---|---|
| 1 | 3 |
| 2 | |

1. *Mian farsh*
2. *Kenareh*
3. *Kellegi*

In the middle of the room, the largest carpet, called the *mian farsh,* is placed. The size varies according to the wealth of the owners, and it can be anything between 5 ft x 12 ft and 9 ft x 24 ft. The mian farsh is the finest carpet in the house and only guests may tread on it. On either side of the mian farsh are *kenarehs* (runners). They vary between 2 ft 6 ins x 12 ft and 3 ft x 24 ft. At the end of the room, on a raised platform, the place for the head of the family, is the *kellegi,* measuring between 4 ft x 5 ft and 5 ft x 10 ft.

Nomads living in tents use a different series of rugs both for bedding and wall coverings. They also use small tent bags and saddle bags for storage which are woven with pile in the same way as ordinary rugs.

Finely knotted Persian carpets are usually made by professionals in the towns and the coarsely-knotted ones by nomads. The professionals had to take into consideration the wishes of their patrons. Finely knotted carpets vary considerably in quality. In modern carpets the warp and weft are usually cotton while the pile is wool. Carpets with a silk pile are rare and rarest of all are those whose warp, weft and pile are all silk. Finely knotted carpets have between 65 and 330 knots per square inch; they appear in all sizes.

Some of the best known Persian carpets are discussed in the following chapters.

# Tabriz

Tabriz in north-western Persia, in the province of Azerbaijan, is the capital of a very important carpet weaving region. The town is over 1000 years old and even centuries ago it was famous as a cultural centre, though now in decline. But still its carpet weaving industry is important; the carpets are of very good quality, finely knotted and made of strong lustrous wool. The colours are soft and attractive. There are old carpets to be found in private homes, used for years, but in excellent condition, and the colours are still bright. Other carpets, called tabriz carpets, use the same design, but the wool is poor and the colours not true. The usual tabriz design is a medallion surrounded by flowers and tendrils; some tabriz carpets have a design with a repeating pattern. The warp and weft are of cotton. There are between 80 and 200 knots to every square inch. The carpets vary in size from 6 ft x 4 ft to 16 ft x 10 ft.

# Heriz

About a day's journey away to the south-east of Tabriz is the town of Heriz. Both Heriz and the nearby town of Georavan, where similar carpets are made, are important centres. Here the carpets are not finely knotted. The patterns are bold, and the pile is thick. Red, blue, ivory, yellow and green are the most common colours. The design is usually a medallion with stylized flowers, and the corners are coloured ivory and blue. On the edges rosettes and leaves alternate. A heriz carpet is easily recognised as it differs from other Persian carpets in colour, shape and knot. Warp and weft are made of cotton. There are between 50 and 100 knots in every square inch. The carpets themselves are usually from 10 ft x 7 ft to 15 ft x 10 ft. Small pieces are rare. Because they are strong and easily cared for they are excellently adapted for use in the house.

*I. Bijar (west Persia).*

*II. Ispahan (central Persia).*

*III. Kurdistan (west Persia).*

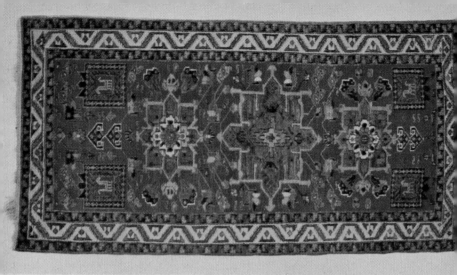

*IV. Heriz (north-west Persia).*　　　　*V. Hamadan (west Persia).*

*VI. Afghan (north Afghanistan).*

*VII.  Kazak (Caucasus).*

*VIII.  Shirvan (Caucasus).*

*IX. Turkish carpet.*

# Feraghan, Mushkabad and Mahal

These carpets are made in the area south of the Caspian Sea, and of them the feraghan carpets are the best known. Very few are made nowadays, and only old ones are to be seen. The herati pattern is found on carpets in many districts of Persia and is the only pattern used on feraghan carpets. The colours are mostly dark, but bright shades appear in the motifs. The knots are quite fine, and the carpet is clipped closely. Since the feraghans were not produced for the European market, they are usually long and narrow, about 6 ft x 12 ft.

The mushkabad, the mahal and the saruk mahal makes are in effect modern feraghans. The mushkabad is the coarsest of these carpets. The saruk is the finest knotted. The mahals are useful in many different kinds of setting since their design and colouring are unobtrusive and they have repeating patterns. White is seldom used; brownish-red with green, blue and yellow are the most common colours. Warp and weft are of cotton. There are between 60 and 140 knots per square inch.

# Sinneh

Sinneh lies to the south of Bijar, and the carpets made there are the finest knotted. Even turkoman carpets cannot be compared with them. Although the wool is not greasy, and sinneh carpets are as a result less shiny than other oriental carpets, they are distinguished by the quality of the classical herati and serabend designs. Sinneh carpets with medallions and squares are also to be found. They are cut very close and are thin, but of extremely good quality. The reverse side is rough because of the sort of knots that are used. The older carpets are much sought after by collectors. Both warp and weft are made of cotton, and there are between 140 and 320 Turkish or ghiordes knots to every square inch. The carpets measure between 5 ft x 4 ft and 10 ft x 6 ft. A few runners are 16 ft x 3 ft.

# Serabend

The serabend had a characteristic pattern consisting of palmettes, or the shawl pattern. Serabends are distinguished by their simplicity. The predominant colour is usually wine-red, though blue or off-white do occur. The finest serabends are called *mir* after the town of Mirabad in the district Serawan. Both warp and weft are made of cotton. On serabends, there are between 55 and 80 knots to every square inch, and on the mir 100 to 220. The carpets are about 6 ft x 4 ft to 11 ft x 8 ft.

# Kashan

The kashan is one of the best Persian carpets. It takes its name from the town of Kashan, which is situated on the caravan route between Teheran and Ispahan. The town was established by Zobeida, who was the favourite wife of the famous Caliph Haroun-al-Raschid. The Ardabil carpets, which were among the most beautiful carpets ever made, were woven by a weaver from Kashan. The knotting is very fine: there are between 120 and 240 knots to each square inch on a woollen kashan and 240 to 550 knots to each square inch on a silk one. The warp and weft are made of cotton or silk. The designs vary from medallions with tendrils to vases, from 'all-over' patterns to very fine flower designs. Red and blue predominate among the pastel shades, and beside them are series of very rich colours that give the kashan a unique appearance. There are also fine kashan rugs with a silk pile. The kashan varies in size from 6 ft x 4 ft to 10 ft x 15 ft.

# Kerman

The town of Kerman is in Eastern Persia, and has always been a centre of the carpet weaving industry. The kermans that come on the market are highly prized because of the

quality of the design and the colours. An old kerman, however, is even better, because of the pastel colours and unique
pattern. They are made of fine, lustrous wool, coloured soft
red, green, blue, yellow and ivory. Both warp and weft are
made of cotton, and there are 130 to 320 knots to every
square inch. The designs vary: the best known is the
medallion carpet with cartouches in the corners and along
the edges. These carpets resemble the French Aubussons. On
the larger kermans there are animal designs or repeating
patterns, the smaller ones often have vase patterns. Certain
small kerman carpets are decorated with portraits of Persian
celebrities and similar pictorial subjects.

# Ispahan

Ispahan was once the capital of Persia, and had the most
beautiful palaces, mosques and libraries. Its golden era was
in the 16th and 17th centuries. Architecture flourished under
Shah Abbas, and so did carpet weaving. The best carpets were
made in his time, and we can see them in museums all over
the world. But very fine well-knotted carpets are still being
produced in Ispahan. The fascinating designs using lines and
arabesques that appear on Islamic architecture also appear
on the modern ispahan carpets. There are flowers on them,
as there are on kashan carpets, but they are discreetly used.
Medallions are the most usual motif, but animals also appear.
Both warp and weft are of cotton. There are between 130
and 360 knots to every square inch. Carpets vary in size from
smaller ones, 6 ft x 4 ft, through the medium sizes, 10 ft x
7 ft or 12 ft x 9 ft up to the larger ones, 12 ft x 10 ft, which
are rare.

# Teheran

Carpets have been made in this town, the capital of Persia,
for centuries. Because Teheran was the capital, the Shah and
the government commissioned many carpets there for use in

public buildings, and as gifts for foreign diplomats. Teheran carpets are among the finest knotted, and they resemble the types that have already been described. The designs include medallions, tendrils and flowers, vases and garden scenes. The dyes used are ivory, red, blue and green; lilac colour is a unique feature of teheran carpets. The warp and weft are both of cotton; there are 160 to 320 knots per square inch, and the carpets vary in size from 6 ft x 5 ft to 8 ft x 5 ft. Large ones measure 10 ft x 7 ft up to 16 ft x 11 ft.

# Qum

In the neighbourhood of Teheran lies the town of Qum, where during the last few decades very good quality carpets have been made. They are finely knotted, and have somewhat compensated for the declining number of old carpets that appear on the market. Qum carpets are dyed striking blue, red and green shades on an ivory background. The designs are derived from classical Persian patterns, such as medallions, animals, gardens, and vases. The warp and weft are both of cotton. There are 120 to 200 knots to a square inch, and the carpets measure 10 ft x 7 ft to 12 ft x 8 ft.

# Meshed and Khorassan

The province of Khorassan lies in the east of Persia, and its capital is Meshed. Khorassan carpets have the same herati pattern as feraghans, but they are dyed a soft purplish-red colour. On feraghans the colours are kept distinct while in khorassans they merge into each other. The wool of a khorassan carpet is much softer than that of a feraghan, and the pile lies flatter, so that the carpet shines more.

Meshed carpets are made of wool that is as soft as that of khorassans, but they resemble kermans in style and colour. Whereas khorassans are rare, masheds are common; but they do not have the beauty or the quality of the kermans and khorassans. The wool is often of inferior quality and, as a result, a meshed is likely to be less strong than a heriz carpet that is much less finely knotted. A star-shaped medallion forms the pattern, and flowers, tendrils and many different borders also appear. The most usual colours are red, blue and green. Both warp and weft are made of cotton. There are 65 to 120 knots per square inch, and the carpets measure 10 ft x 7 ft to 18 ft x 11 ft.

There are two qualities of meshed carpet, the farsibaff and the turkibaff, one made with a Persian knot and one with a Turkish knot. The farsibaffs are the most common.

## Saruk

Saruk is a town in Central Persia, near Hamadan; the old carpets from this town are among the best ever made. They are distinguished by their colours and glossy wool. The designs are varied, and medallions with herati pattern on the edge, as well as carpets with an 'all-over' design, like ferag-hans, are commonly found. Old saruks are finely knotted and thin, but they are very strong, so that some 19th century carpets have survived and are still in good condition. A modern saruk has thicker pile, but it is well knotted and very solid. There are between 100 and 260 knots per square inch; both warp and weft are made of cotton. Saruks vary in size from 6 ft x 5 ft to 7 ft x 5 ft and 10 ft x 7 ft to 16 ft x 8 ft.

## Mosul

Although Mosul is in Iraq, not Persia, on the right bank of the Tigris, the name was given to certain kinds of rugs made in the villages around Hamadan. Mostly these rugs were made by Kurds, and they are difficult to describe be-cause they vary considerably. They cannot be recognised by their patterns because these also vary.

Mosul carpets are to be recognised by the finish of the work and the quality of the wool. Usually they are coarsely knotted and as a result the patterns are not entirely symmetrical. Mosuls are made entirely of wool; the pile is very long, glossy sheep's wool, camel-hair or goat's hair. The wool used for warp and weft is usually dark brown or black and coarse. The selvedges may help one to recognise the carpet as a mosul, because they are thickly covered with different coloured wools. There is a fringe only at one end of the carpet. At the other end is a band of plain weaving terminating in the loops by which the warp was attached to the loom.

Mosuls are cheap, but thick, pleasant to walk on and extremely strong. They are made only in small sizes, and the largest are 5 ft x 7 ft. Occasionally a mosul is found with really distinguished colours, and some of the old camel bags are very fine indeed.

# Hamadan

Camel-hair dominates hamadan carpets, for the basic colour was usually the beige of camel-hair. Sometimes in ancient times a pattern was woven by using two slightly different shades of camel-hair. The usual design is a central medallion set against the beige background, and a fairly broad border. The pattern is not finely drawn, and even looks clumsy, but the charm of a hamadan lies in the colour. The beautiful red, blue and green shades, with touches of white, combine with the ground colour to give much the same impression as the windows of a Gothic cathedral. The older hamadans are particularly attractive. Little camel-hair is used in modern hamadans but they can easily be recognised because of the characteristic reverse side. The warp and weft are both made of white cotton, and warp threads sometimes pass over three weft threads. As a result the reverse side shows short white stripes.

Usually the hamadans are even heavier and more closely woven than the mosuls or village rugs. They are very strong indeed. They vary in size from 5 ft x 3 ft to 8 ft x 5 ft. Large hamadans are rare. Runners are 10 ft x 2 ft 6 ins to 20 ft x 3 ft.

# Kurdistan

Kurdistan carpets resemble hamadans, but they are much thicker and heavier. Whereas hamadans can be folded, a kurdistan carpet must be rolled. Women and girls make these tightly-knotted carpets, in spite of their weight.

It is true that there are some softer kurdistan carpets, but in general one can say that, if a rug cannot be folded and lies like a board on the floor, it is either a kurdistan or a bijar. The latter are shorn close and the pile stands stiffly upright. The pile of a kurdistan carpet lies flat.

There are two patterns commonly used for kurdistan carpets: these are the rosette-motif and the long medallion motif, as in the hamadan. Vases often appear in the central design. The wool is glossy and dyed attractive brown, red, dark-blue and ivory colours. The carpets vary in size from 6 ft x 4 ft to 10 ft x 5 ft.

# Bijar

Bijar is a town in the west of Persia in Kurdistan. The heaviest carpets are made at Bijar. When a woman has tied a row of knots and thrown several shoots of the weft, a man using a heavy comb beats the rows of knots together. As a result, the carpets are so stiff and tight that they cannot be folded, and are practically indestructible. The warp and pile are all made of sheep's wool or camel-hair. The most usual designs are of medallions, small scattered flowers and decorated corners. The borders are finely drawn and have an individual appearance. Some bijars have repeating patterns. Bijar carpets are very hard-wearing and therefore suitable for hotel lounges and similar rooms. There are 100 to 160 knots to every square inch. The carpets vary in size from 6 ft x 4 ft to 8 ft x 5 ft and 10 ft x 6 ft to 24 ft x 13 ft 6 ins.

# Shiraz

All the nomad carpets that have so far been described are made in Northern and Western Persia. But shiraz carpets are made in the South. Shiraz has been known for centuries as the city of roses, and, although the rose gardens are gone, the roses live on in the carpets. Other patterns are, however, used; among them appear motifs such as very stylised human and animal figures. Shiraz is the capital of the large province of Fars. There are four main groups of nomads whose rugs are marketed in Shiraz though no rugs are made in the city.

Shiraz carpets are loosely knotted and therefore very supple. The wool is soft and glossy, so that a good quality shiraz carpet is reminiscent of an animal's skin.

A shiraz can be recognised by the selvedges which are finished off with coloured wool so as to form a sort of cord. Often the selvedges are decorated with colourful tassels. The webs at the ends of the rugs are often attractively embroidered; old carpets are more often embroidered than modern ones.

Only the very best shiraz should be used on the floor where they would receive any appreciable wear since they are very soft. Warp and weft threads are wool or goat's hair. Among the better known of the individual tribal rugs are those made by the Qashqai, and by the Persian village of Abadeh. Sometimes grouped with them are the rugs made by the Afshari who are not part of this group but market their rugs through Kerman.

Shiraz carpets are made in all sizes; 4 ft x 2 ft 6 ins, 5 ft x 4 ft, 7 ft x 5 ft and 10 ft x 7 ft. Square shiraz are also to be found.

# Bakhtiari

Rugs made in the district of Chahar Mahal, south-west of Ispahan, are called by this name because the district was settled by Khans from the Bakhtiari tribe. These carpets have bright colours with flower motifs in various designs together with medallion carpets and blocks in which stylised trees and

plants are drawn. Old 'bakhtiari' carpets, which are beautifully designed and coloured, are very scarce. Modern 'bakhtiari' are rather too bright, but they are good quality carpets.
There are between 50 and 130 knots to a square inch.
Warp and weft are made of cotton. The carpets vary in size
from 7 ft x 4 ft and 10 ft x 6 ft to 15 ft x 12 ft.

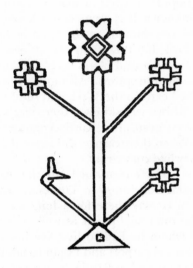

# Turkoman carpets

Baluchi and afghan carpets are very remarkable carpets, similar to each other, but with some great differences. They are extremely popular carpets in some western countries, but were almost unknown fifty years ago, whereas Turkish and Persian carpets were famous in the West as long ago as the 17th century. Probably turkoman carpets were unknown in the West because Central Asia itself was mysterious and seldom visited by Europeans. Although Turkestan's name was occasionally heard in the West, and the Emir of Bokhara and the Khan Khiwa were known, there was little talk about them in the West even after Russia conquered them about 130 years ago. When their carpets did reach the West, nobody knew where they had come from.

This state of affairs continued till the Russian government sent General Bogolubow to Turkestan with instructions that caused him to stay there for a long time. The general happened to be interested in art as well as in the life of the people among whom he had to live. He became aware that they made very good carpets and began to admire and collect them. When he returned to Russia, he wrote a richly illustrated book in two volumes, published in 1908 in Russian and French, bearing the title *Les tapis de l'Asie Centrale*. Our knowledge of Turkestan carpets begins with General Bogolubow and his work has been surpassed by no one since.

Turkestan carpets are made in the area round the sea of Aral and the area between China and the Caspian Sea, Siberia in the north, and India, Pakistan and Persia in the south. The population is very mixed, but the most numerous section is of Turkish origin, and there are many Mongol people. There are several groups of Turkoman tribes all of whom made carpets: the Salor, Tekke and Saryq group, the Yomud group (which includes the Chodors), the Afghans who lived on both sides of the border between Turkestan and Afghanistan, and the Ersari. These peoples were formerly nomadic shepherds and hunters and they lived by rearing cattle, fishing, and hunting. Trade and agriculture were unimportant. But conquest by the Russians has led many of the people to settle down and farm. The rugs made by these people provided the basic furniture for their dwellings, tents called 'kibitkas', made with a wooden frame. This is covered on the outside with felt and on the inside with pieces of matting. The kibitkas are cylindrical and the roof is blunt and coneshaped. The ground is covered with thick felt, and along the walls are spaces for sleeping.

In the middle of the floor is always the one large carpet to be found, measuring about 6 ft x 10 ft. All domestic life is played out on that carpet. On it stands the simple loom where the carpets and bags are made either for household use or the daughters' dowries.

Along the walls, where people sleep, are smaller carpets that are soft and supple as animal skins. Since there are no forests in Central Asia, only steppe lands and occasional bare hills, there is no wood for furniture. Clothing, household articles and weapons are stored in bags hanging on the wall. The bags are made using the same technique as the carpets. They are small carpets whose reverse side is simply woven wool. The bags are designed to hold particular articles, so that those intended for guns or long swords are long and narrow, and decorated with a fringe.

The entrance to the tent is shut off by a door rug called a 'namazlyq'. Its design is rather similar to that of a prayer rug though it resembles also the panels of a door, inlaid with ivory after being richly carved. Fundamentally the design is a cross enriched with the decoration appropriate to each tribe.

Long bands of woven material with knotted decoration on a plain ground are used in and on the kibitkas. They may strengthen its structure and exclude draughts and they are highly decorative. The colours and patterns are often most attractive.

Although turkoman carpets differ, they have certain

characteristics in common. The principal colour is always a warm red. Modern carpets are dyed with synthetic dyes, but the old colour schemes of turkoman carpets seem to be specially designed to show off the beautiful red. Sometimes it has a purplish tinge, sometimes it is brownish.

The pattern of turkoman carpets is also distinctive. They are geometrical, consisting of rows of frames, hexagons or octagons. These figures are called 'gul' which means 'rose' in Persian. Each tribal group has its own gul which is quite distinctive and so it is possible to tell who made a rug by looking at the gul. There are few plant or animal motifs, although the makers of the carpets spend all their time in contact with nature.

Turkoman carpets can also be recognised by the treatment of the web at the ends of the carpets. This web tends to be much broader on turkoman than on other carpets and it is often elaborately decorated. Sometimes it is made in one colour only, often it is striped and quite often it is embroidered as well.

Turkoman and afghan carpets can be up to 6 ft x 10 ft in size. Some of the finest are made by the Tekke tribe. Since they are exported from Bokhara the name of the city has often been used in the carpet trade as a generic (though incorrect) term for all turkoman rugs. No carpets are actually made in the town itself. Often there are 160 to 260 knots to each square inch on a turkoman carpet, and only the finest Persian carpets can compete with this. Turkoman rugs made in the late 19th century are often soft and glossy. The wool is thin, supple and strong but the dyes by this date are not as good as those in carpets made a generation earlier.

Afghan rugs are coarser than turkoman rugs. Their rugs contain about 100 knots to each square inch, and the carpets are highly thought of, particularly if they were made between 1850 and 1900. The colours are rich, the patterns bold and the carpets themselves are very durable.

Although the Baluchi tribes are not Turkomans and their geographical home is far from that of the Turkoman tribes their rugs are usually classified with this group because they are so similar. Dark blue is often the most important colour

44

but red is common. The patterns of baluchistan carpets are less geometrical and the gul is more naturalistic. Animal and flower motifs are common. Old baluchistan carpets are particularly attractive because of the glossy wool, suppleness and lack of rigidity in the pattern. There are usually about 65 knots to a square inch, and the carpets are seldom bigger than 6 ft x 10 ft. The most beautiful baluchistans are found among the smaller pieces.

Modern turkoman carpets are mainly woven either in the USSR or in Pakistan and tribal distinctions in their patterns have become blurred. There is a difference between the two groups. Those made in the USSR tend to copy old patterns rather closely, on a much reduced scale, using a bright tomato red. Pakistan 'turkomans' tend to have simpler patterns on a rather larger scale with a softer, richer red. Baluchistan rugs are still made in Persia.

# Caucasian carpets

A wide range of beautiful rugs and carpets has come to Europe from the Caucasus. These were generally woven by women. Their rugs were well woven with strong wool and good dyes. The Caucasus, which is now part of the USSR, contains a great mixture of peoples — Turks, Armenians, Persians and Georgians, Circassians, Tartars, and Kurds. The region is divided by the Caucasus mountains. This range and the many rivers and smaller mountains help to break up the area. In the past, each district produced a characteristic pattern or type of rug, though frequent migration and inter-marriage blurred the picture. Some features are common to all Caucasian carpets, their woollen warp, weft and pile and their texture, rather coarser than those from Asia Minor. Camel-hair and silk are seldom used.

Patterns are chiefly geometrical except the *karabaghs* which have much more naturalistic floral patterns, owing to the close proximity of the district to Persia. Normally motifs are angular and formed from straight lines. Graceful curved lines like those in Persian carpets do not occur. In the pattern are blocks, rectangles, checks, hexagons, octagons, stars, etc. Human and animal figures, so stylised that they are geometrical shapes, are also to be found. They look somewhat grotesque and give a comic touch to the stern geometrical pattern.

The patterns are usually arranged in straight lines, or in

diagonals, or next to one another without any link between them.

The colours of Caucasian carpets contrast sharply with those of turkoman rugs because they are so variegated. Cream, red and blue are the chief colours, and black, brown and green appear in addition. The older Caucasian carpets were dyed using vegetable dyes, but the newer rugs are dyed with chemical dyes.

Thick Caucasian carpets with a deep pile are mostly made in the north of the country. In the south, the carpets are more finely knotted and thinner. Both sorts are small in size. Only the sumaks are sometimes as big as 8 ft x 11 ft. 3 ft x 5 ft to 5 ft x 7 ft is a more usual size. Kazaks are sometimes as big as 6 ft x 10 ft.

The carpets woven in the Caucasus in the 18th—19th century can be grouped into about ten to twelve types each originating in one area. The newer carpets, however, are not so easily distinguished as the older ones, and there have always been different intermediate types.

The *kazak* is a very well known Caucasian carpet and a few old kazak rugs are still exported to the West. The region lies between Georgia and Armenia in the western Caucasus. Kazak rugs tend to be heavier and thicker than any other Caucasian carpets; they last for a long while even if they are laid on the floor. Blue and red are the principal colours;

cream, black and brown are used for the contours. A dark grass green is sometimes substituted for the blue. The patterns are large and boldly drawn. The most usual pattern is one to three large medallions in blue set against a dark red background. This arrangement may be reversed. Both the medallions and the ground colour are filled in with very varied and asymmetrical small angular motifs. The carpets as a whole are more or less symmetrical.

The patterns of kazak rugs may vary considerably. Two patterns which are particularly common are a design, perhaps based originally on a cloud band, which is composed from S-shaped motifs and the design based on star-shaped medallions.

There are 55 to 120 knots to a square inch. Usually a kazak measures about 5 ft x 7 ft.

The *shirvan* carpet is another very handsome Caucasian type. The newer ones are sometimes badly made. Shirvan is a region immediately to the south of the Caucasian mountains and lies between them and the river Kura. The region extends to the coast on which there is the important city of Baku. In this region there are several villages and towns which once produced quite distinctive carpets of their own. Thus shirvan carpets have extremely varied designs. Some resemble the kazaks although the medallions are smaller. There are far more of the small motifs than appear in the kazaks, and pale pastel shades are used. Pink, yellow and ivory appear as well as the colours used in kazaks. In older carpets the warp and weft were, of course, wool but cotton is found in the newer carpets. Shirvans are very finely knotted; there are between 65 and 200 knots to a square inch. They vary in size from 4 ft x 2 ft 6 ins to 6 ft x 4 ft. Larger sizes are rare.

*9. Kashaï (south Persia).*

*10. Shiraz (south Persia).*

*11. Hatchli-afghan (north Afghanistan).*

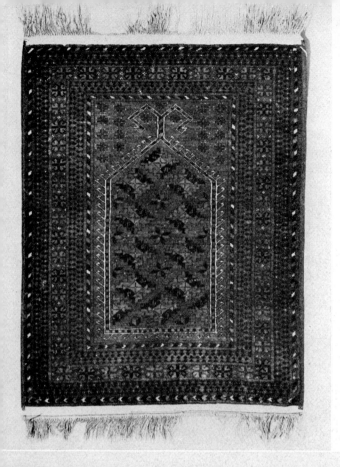

12. *Afghan prayer r*
13. *Bokhara*
*( Turkestan, central A*

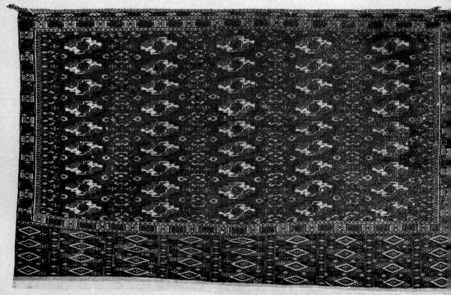

*14. Baluchistan (borders of east Persia).*

*15. Mosul donkey bag.*        *16. Shiraz donkey bag.*

*17. Baluchi camel bag.*

*18. Traditional Chinese carpet.*

19. Morrocan carpet made from sheep's wool.
20. Detail of 19.

*Kabistan* carpets are made in the Baku area, and resemble shirvans closely. The chief colour is usually blue, and the typical motifs are angular and light.

*Tchitchi* carpets are made in a village south-east of Kuba and are similar to shirvans but can be recognised by their broad inner border of rosettes and slanting logs. These carpets are rare.

The *karabaghs* are made on the borders of Persia and the Caucasus, and they show clearly the influence of kazaks as well as of Persian carpets. The borders are usually straight, like those of the kazaks. In the centre field are large checks, patterns or medallions with flowers inside. Although karabaghs are not stylistically pure and they keep their own identity, they resemble most closely the Caucasian carpets in technique and colour arrangement. They are valued accordingly.

Some karabaghs were made, probably on commission from Frenchmen or other Europeans, in the style of Aubusson carpets and with French designs.

The karabagh is a good quality carpet, with strong wool that is less glossy than that of the kazaks. There are 50 to 100 knots per square inch. A karabagh usually measures 6 ft x 4 ft to 10 ft x 5 ft.

*Sumak* rugs appear to have taken their name from the town (today called Shemakha) but were woven all over the Caucasus especially in Dagestan. They are very strong because of their double texture even though they do not have any pile.

The patterns of sumak rugs are generally treated very boldly with motifs in contrasting colours, red and blue predominating. Octagons and the normal range of Caucasian decoration — rosettes, small stylised animals and men — appear in sumak rugs as in pile carpets. The newer sumak may, if it is badly woven, have very bright and unattractive orange or yellow colouring. Old sumaks, if they are well woven, are valuable possessions.

All Caucasian carpets are made with a Turkish knot.

# Turkish carpets

Turkish carpets include those woven in Turkey and those in Asia Minor. Some of the peoples who wove carpets in the past were not of Turkish origin so designs varied considerably. Plant motifs and animals are rare because the Turks were very orthodox Moslems and followers of Mohammed were forbidden to portray living creatures. Turkish motifs were usually geometrical, or very stylised flower designs.

The warp and weft in Turkish carpets is generally cotton. The wool used for the pile is rather soft and often without much sheen. Cotton is also sometimes used quite extensively in the pile — especially to make the white parts of a design. Ghiordes prayer rugs often are woven with such effects. Turkish carpets are, of course, woven with a Turkish knot. With the exception of the court carpets made at the end of the 19th century, Turkish carpets are not as finely knotted as Persian ones.

Carpets have been made for centuries in Asia Minor. Apart from the Pazyrik carpet, some fragments found in the Burying Grounds of Egypt (at Akmim and Antinoë) and some found in the rubbish heaps along the old silk route from China the oldest carpets come from Asia Minor. Some of the best preserved are from the Mosque at Konia, a town where carpets are made to this day.

The first carpets to be exported to the West came from Asia Minor and they can be seen depicted in Italian paintings from the 13th century onwards. By the 15th century they were being exported to northern Europe and consequently appear in Flemish paintings. Cardinal Wolsey — and Henry VIII — both imported Turkish carpets in quantity from Venice. In England all oriental carpets were called 'turkey carpets' as a matter of course and upholstery made in the same way in England was called 'turkey work'. The first knotted carpets to be made in western Europe, in Spain in the 15th century and in the late 16th century in England, were woven in patterns copied from Turkish carpets. The octagons and mock kufic (an angular form of the arabic script) where imitated in rather different colours. Only in the 17th century did Persian carpets begin to come to Western Europe, imported by the Dutch, English and French East India Companies. Gradually, an increasing number of Persian carpets appears in paintings of the 17th century but the splendid *ushak* carpets from Turkey continue to hold their own until nearly the end of the 17th century. Many rugs were exported from Smyrna and in some countries 'Smyrna rugs' became synonymous with Turkish carpets — even though they might have been woven in Ushak, Isparta, Konia or elsewhere. Rugs were made for special markets too — and one group, the 'Transylvanian' carpets have been found in great numbers in this part of Europe. These too appear in paintings of the 17th and 18th century.

A large number of fine early Turkish carpets have survived and are preserved in the museum collections of most countries. In Sweden there are a number of the earliest, rather angular, stylised, animal rugs dating from the late 15th century and early 16th century. (These survived chiefly in churches, for the Swedish Reformation was not as violent as that elsewhere and their collections were left undisturbed.) 16th century 'Holbein rugs' are very rare but ushak rugs and carpets woven in red and blue chiefly with large medallions on a contrasting ground can be seen in London, New York, Berlin, Paris, Vienna and, indeed, in most capital cities. 18th century Turkish carpets are more widely scattered still — there are many good ones in the United States.

Several Turkish sultans had special centres where hundreds of women and children worked under the direction of professional craftsmen. The last sultan, Abdul Hamid, had his own workshops at Hereke. Carpets such as these were of excellent quality and they are now in museums, or in collections. One square yard of a very good 17th century carpet costs £300 ($850.00).

Because sultans needed a constant supply of carpets for

courtesans, favourites and visitors from the West, practically all royal palaces in the occident have some very fine Turkish carpets.

Carpets are still made in Turkey in many places but the quality seldom compares with that of old carpets. Among the best known carpets of the late 19th and early 20th century are the following:

*Smyrna.* Coarsely woven carpet with cotton warp and weft. The design is open. Before the Second World War they were sometimes seen in hotels or private homes but they were not of good quality.

*Sparta.* The name refers to Isparta in Western Asia Minor. Many different designs were used here, both from Turkish and Persian origin. Old carpets made at Isparta were quite attractive and of good quality.

*Sivas.* Like the sparta it was an imitation of the Turkish and Persian carpets. The sivas were more finely knotted and resembled closely an old tebriz or kashan.

*Hereke.* The sultan's workshop was once here. Very fine carpets were made at Hereke, with classical designs. Prayer rugs were also made. Hereke carpets were often made of silk, and may be large or small.

Although it is impossible to give details of all the old and antique carpets made in Turkey, the following are the best known varieties which were made up to the beginning of the 20th century.

The *ghiordes* is the most famous, a prayer rug with an open 'mihrab'. It often has a design with a lamp on the upper side and the colours are green and ivory.

The *kula* resembles the ghiordes. There are two main kinds of pattern in the classic kula rugs. In one the mihrab is supported on two columns on a plain field. In the other the central field is covered with rows of flowers and the borders are composed of many narrow stripes. This kind of rug is comparatively common.

The *ladik* is usually a prayer rug with a row of stylised tulips on a bar underneath the mihrab. The tulip originated in Asia Minor and the flower appears on Rhodes and Isnik pottery.

The *bergama* was very popular. It resembles the Caucasian carpets, looks rather primitive, and differs in shape and colour from the Turkish carpets we have mentioned. The pattern is usually confined to red and blue with only a little white, yellow or any other colour. The bergama has Turkish motifs, which are stylised and usually drawn round one or more medallions.

The *kis-bergama* is usually about one yard square; it was made by young girls for their 'bottom drawer' or hope chest and is usually coloured blue.

Among the classic Turkish carpets the *melas* and *mujur* are important. The *panderma* and *yuruk* are two modern types of rug. The *saph* is a type of long, narrow rug with a number of prayer niches woven side by side.

A beautiful collection of carpets from Asia Minor can be viewed upon request at the New York Metropolitan Museum of Art.

# Chinese carpets

Chinese carpets are easily distinguished because they differ in colour and pattern from all other sorts. But the same wool, the same threads for making warp and weft, the same knot, the same simple loom and the same methods were used by Chinese carpet weavers as by other craftsmen.

Chinese porcelain, Chinese bronzes and painting have been famous for centuries in the West but the first carpets probably came during the 19th century, perhaps after the sack of the summer palace in Pekin in 1860. The craft of carpet weaving is no novelty in the Far East; The Imperial Treasury in Japan has the oldest remaining Chinese carpets, and they are more than 1000 years old.

Carpets have probably been made in the region now called Chinese Turkestan for the past 2000 years. Early literary sources indicate that carpets of high quality came from this region but the earliest surviving carpets are not older than the 19th century. They are distinctive in colouring and pattern owing something to China and something to Central Asia. These carpets are quite different from those made in China for the Chinese court. Old Chinese carpets were made for temples and palaces, and they were most commonly intended for use on the floor, on the altar or as curtains or baldachin. Some carpets were used to cover pillars, and these usually bore a dragon which seemed to coil itself round the pillar. They are quite different from any other known carpet.
Chinese carpets are made in the same technique as other oriental rugs. Sometimes they are knotted with a Turkish knot in the borders and a Persian knot in the central field. When compared with a Persian carpet a Chinese one looks angular and clean cut, so that the effect is as of mosaic. This

effect is not achieved only by knotting very finely, but also by using certain knacks. Compared with a turkoman or kashan, a Chinese carpet is not closely woven. The Chinese craftsmen achieved the effect of relief by shaving out the edges of the pattern and sometimes, also, certain colours, more deeply than the rest. Furthermore the Chinese did not allow wool at the edge of one colour section to become mixed with different coloured wool: instead, each piece of wool is combed so that it lies with wool of its own colour, using a long fine needle. As a result the scales on a dragon's tail will each stand out distinctly, and so will its whiskers, its eye, as well as the pupil of the eye.

Chinese carpet patterns are the same as those on vases, bronzes and silken material; the motifs are much older than the carpets. Chinese carpets, alone among all the different kinds of oriental rug, do not have their own decorative scheme. They are very easy therefore to distinguish from the carpets of every other eastern country but very difficult to date. Each motif in the design may have a symbolic meaning, so that a dragon indicates immortality, and imperial power if the animal has five claws instead of four. The red ball in front of the dragon indicates thunder and lightning. The cloud band (Tschi) which is also called the holy Fungus of the Chinese, is the seat of divinity as well as the life symbol. The Yang-Yin symbol indicates the primeval powers controlling all life and the dualism which controls all existence.

Chinese carpets are well-made and hard wearing, the better quality products are heavier than the heaviest rug from Bijar or Kurdistan. Many Chinese carpets have recently been on the market that are coloured grey, beige and soft powder blue shades. Others are in one colour only, some with a simple border with a restful self-coloured pattern cut in the pile.

Chinese carpets measure from about 8 ft x 5 ft to 13 ft x 10 ft.

# Moroccan carpets

The Maghrib belongs, as does Asia Minor, to the Mo-hammedan world, and Moroccan carpets, which seldom receive attention in books on oriental carpets, deserve it on both artistic and historical grounds.

Morocco is peopled by many different groups, but the earliest known inhabitants were Berbers. The Berbers in Morocco mostly work on the land or rear sheep, and some of them are nomads. Each Berber group has its own carpet design, which differs in pattern, colour and technique from all others. At least twenty types have been distinguished.

In *Rabat* the carpets are made and used by town dwellers; the carpets are adapted to the Arab house, and appear more sophisticated than other Moroccan carpets. Such carpets look like those from Asia Minor, especially the bergama, for they share many motifs with the carpets of Anatolia. As in Asia Minor, red madder, cochineal, and in the small motifs, most colours are used.

The carpets from the *little Atlas* area are more typically Moroccan. The knots are so large that they can be seen with the naked eye; the carpets are not clipped, so that the pile is long and the pattern not clear. If the main colour is white, which is often the case, the carpets look like large fleeces. Probably fleeces were used before carpets to protect people from the cold and damp. Modern Moroccans certainly do sleep on these carpets.

The patterns are simple and very decorative, and white, black or dark brown are the most usual colours. It is rare that one finds a Berber carpet with a border, but a simple one is occasionally seen. Both sides of the carpets are regarded as equally useful; in the summer the smooth side is uppermost, and in the winter the pile is on top.

Near *Marrakesh* carpets are made with bold, childlike patterns, using a magnificent garnet red. Moroccan carpets are becoming more and more popular. They can be obtained on order or from stock and are available in more than sixty shades, and in original Berber designs.

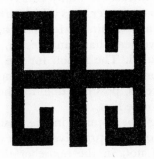

# Prayer rugs

In 1939 every carpet dealer would have had at least twelve prayer rugs, usually fine old ones, in his stock, but even modern ones are now almost unobtainable. The demand for them has, however, continued for they are often of good quality and very attractive. Many collections and ordinary private houses boast prayer rugs which are, more than any other variety of carpet, suitable for hanging on the wall for they are of a convenient shape and design, carefully knotted and warmly coloured. The reason for the disappearance of the prayer rug from the market is something of a mystery but the disappearance is possibly due to the penetration of Western culture to the East.

The prayer rug was popular in the East because all Mohammedans are bound to pray five times a day, preferably in a mosque, but if not, in the house or the open air. The Moslem must kneel down and bow his forehead several times to the ground, while he is facing Mecca. In the mosque, on the wall facing Mecca, is a niche called the 'mihrab', where the man stands who leads the people in prayer. The mihrab indicates the direction towards which the faithful must face. A Moslem who is travelling may be glad to be reminded of the mihrab, so most prayer rugs have in their design a niche similar to that of the style of the particular country. For this reason prayer rugs are the only oriental carpets that are asymmetrical.

In some Moslem countries, in Java, for example, the faithful pray on ordinary mats, or kneel on the ground. Moroccan Moslems never use prayer rugs. Persians use pressed cotton or embroidered silk mats, though they also have finely knotted ones as well, if they can afford them.

The best prayer rugs are from Asia Minor, particularly Anatolia.

# How to care for oriental carpets

Oriental carpets should not be professionally cleaned more often than once a year. They may be cleaned every day with a vacuum cleaner but never beaten. Once a week the floor under the carpet may be swept. Such precautions should be sufficient to protect the carpet against moths. Only suitable insecticides should be used and the manufacturer's instructions should be followed strictly.

When a carpet has been exposed to wear and tear for some time, the selvedges and the fringes are damaged first, and should be repaired as soon as possible. At this stage, repairs are inexpensive, but if the warp threads are damaged, an entirely new selvedge may be required and this is generally a task for a professional restorer. If a hole has appeared in the carpet, new warp and weft threads will be needed before the pile can be rewoven. It is often difficult to find wool that matches that which was used on an old carpet, and old wool only is suitable. An expert can choose the right colour, which can easily be incorporated in a coarsely knotted carpet, but only with very great difficulty worked into a fine turkoman or kashan carpet.

An oriental carpet may be washed in water, provided the colours are each first tested individually and found to be fast. The carpet should be dried within a few days for if it is left for too long while wet or even damp, it may develop mildew. This can damage the warp and weft. Soap or a mild detergent can be used. If the carpet is a valuable one, the owner may be well advised to seek professional advice before cleaning it by any method. Damaged antique carpets are kept behind glass. Unwary buyers should be careful to ensure that they are not sold damaged carpets at auction sales.

# How to buy oriental carpets and rugs

An oriental carpet often may last a lifetime, and it is best to think carefully before choosing one. But nomad carpets, in particular, are seldom quite perfect in design and it is unwise to look for mistakes in the carpets that are for sale. An old carpet may have one or two bare patches, but be well repaired and still a great acquisition. To avoid making disastrous mistakes, it is best to buy from a well-known firm. A reputable firm will usually change a carpet which, though newly bought, is obviously damaged.

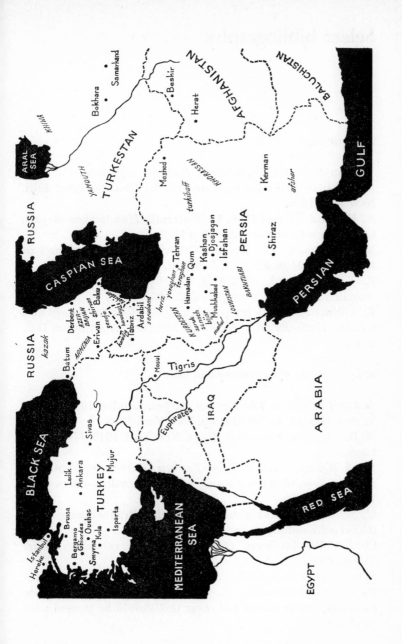

# Select bibliography

### Antique rugs

W. von Bode and E. Kühnel, *Antique rugs from the Near East*, 4th revised edition, translated by Charles Grant Ellis. New York 1958.

A. F. Kendrick and C. E. C. Tattersall, *Handwoven carpets, Oriental and European*. London 1922.

M. S. Dimand, *The Ballard Collection of oriental rugs in the City Art Museum of St. Louis*. St. Louis 1935.

E. Kühnel and L. Bellinger, *Catalogue of Spanish Rugs*. Textile Museum, Washington D.C. 1953.

E. Kühnel and L. Bellinger, *Catalogue of Cairene Rugs and others technically related*. Textile Museum, Washington D.C. 1957.

### Rugs from the 19th century and later

A. Cecil Edwards, *The Persian Carpet*. London 1953.

Walter Hawley, *Oriental Rugs*. New York 1913.

A. B. Thacher, *Turkoman Rugs*. New York 1940 (Hajo Baba Club).

Hans Bidder, *Carpets from Eastern Turkestan, known as Khotan, Samarkand and Kansu Carpets*. London — New York 1964.

U. Schürmann, *Kaukasische Teppiche*. Braunschweig 1961. (Good coloured plates and a map.)

Charles W. Jacobsen, *Oriental Rugs, a complete guide*. Tokyo 1962.

(There are several similar comprehensive books dealing with the carpets in the trade. They are useful, especially, as a guide to current trade names but their text should be treated with caution.)

## Technique

There are chapters on technique in most of the books mentioned in the first section.

C. E. C. Tattersall, *Notes on carpet knotting and weaving.* Victoria and Albert Museum, London, H.M.S.O.